EARTH IN ACTION

WILDFIRES

by Rebecca Rowell

Content Consultant
Jennifer Rivers Cole, PhD
Department of Earth & Planetary Sciences
Harvard University

CORE
LIBRARY

Published by ABDO Publishing Company, PO Box 398166, Minneapolis, MN 55439. Copyright © 2014 by Abdo Consulting Group, Inc. International copyrights reserved in all countries. No part of this book may be reproduced in any form without written permission from the publisher. The Core Library™ is a trademark and logo of ABDO Publishing Company.

Printed in the United States of America,
North Mankato, Minnesota
042013
112013

Editor: Mirella Maxwell
Series Designer: Becky Daum

Library of Congress Control Number: 2013932509

Cataloging-in-Publication Data
Rowell, Rebecca.
 Wildfires / Rebecca Rowell.
   p. cm. -- (Earth in action)
ISBN 978-1-61783-943-6 (lib. bdg.)
ISBN 978-1-62403-008-6 (pbk.)
1. Wildfires--Juvenile literature. 2. Natural disasters--Juvenile literature. I. Title.
363.37--dc23

                                    2013932509

Photo Credits: iStockphoto/Thinkstock, cover, 1, 12, 14, 30, 38; Bryan Oller/AP Images, 4, 45; Jerilee Bennett/The Colorado Springs Gazette/AP Images, 7; Ed Andrieski/AP Images, 8; Red Line Editorial, Inc., 16; Hemera/Thinkstock, 17; Steve Malone/Santa Barbara News-Press/AP Images, 19; RJ Sangosti/Denver Post/AP Images, 20; Shutterstock Images, 23; Jupiterimages/Thinkstock, 24; Chris Carlson/AP Images, 26; Ted S. Warren/AP Images, 29; Jim Ross/NASA/AP Images, 32; Jason Patrick Ross/Shutterstock Images, 34; Dan Cepeda/The Casper Star-Tribune/AP Images, 36; Nick Ut/AP Images, 40

CONTENTS

CHAPTER ONE

COLORADO BURNING

Residents of Waldo Canyon, Colorado, waited anxiously for news of the fire spreading through their community. Some wondered if they would have to evacuate the area. Others had already fled and wanted to know what was left of their homes.

On June 22, 2012, local city officials received a report of smoke in Waldo Canyon. Investigators went to the reported scene and searched until nightfall but

The 2012 Waldo Canyon Fire burned thousands of acres of land before it was finally contained.

found nothing. They returned the next day to find fire raging. Winds fueled the flames and pushed them into residential areas, including Colorado Springs, Colorado.

The fire grew rapidly and was soon threatening homes. Winds blew, sometimes gusting as high as 65 miles per hour (105 km/h). Black smoke filled the air, and clouds glowed orange, reflecting the flames that raged below. The wildfire destroyed blocks of houses.

On June 26, officials ordered 32,000 residents to evacuate. Given little time—sometimes only an hour—people grabbed only the most important and prized possessions from their homes. Vehicles packed, they joined the jammed roads to escape the fire rapidly heading toward their properties. Some stayed with friends and family in communities not affected by the fire. Others found safety in shelters.

Evacuees did not know if flames would reach their homes or if they would ever return to their properties

Thousands of residents in the Colorado Springs area were unsure when they would be returning home.

and belongings. In the end, a few hundred people never saw their homes again.

Colorado's Worst Fire

The Waldo Canyon Fire dominated local and national news for weeks. Newscasters reported daily on its

The Waldo Canyon Fire destroyed more than 340 homes in its destructive path.

status, telling viewers of its terrible destruction while showing images of burning trees and properties. There was so much fire.

For weeks firefighters battled the blaze in an effort to contain its flames. Hundreds of emergency workers joined the effort.

Firefighters finally contained the Waldo Canyon Fire on July 10. By that time, the wildfire had burned

18,247 acres (7 ha)—close to 28 square miles (72 sq km)—of land. The destruction included more than 340 homes. An elderly couple died in the blaze. It was the worst fire in Colorado history.

Common Natural Disaster

The devastating blaze in Waldo Canyon was not Colorado's first wildfire. It was not even the first wildfire in the state that year. The Waldo Canyon Fire was one of several that burned in 2012. As the massive wildfire swept through Waldo Canyon in late June, seven other large fires burned in the state. For a while, flames seemed to engulf the entire state—Colorado was on fire.

More Fires Expected

Researchers believe wildfires are going to increase per year. Regions where wildfires already occur regularly are expected to double their burned area. The central part of the United States, from North Dakota to Texas, will experience climate changes making them more susceptible to wildfires. They will likely become drier as a result of the warming climate and dangerous greenhouse gases.

Wildfires are common in Colorado, but they are not unique to that state. They also occur in other parts of the United States and on other continents, including Europe and Asia.

Wildfires occur under certain conditions. They have specific causes and undeniable effects, but not all wildfires are negative. Some scientists study wildfires to better understand them. They use their studies to help people prevent—or at least limit—the kind of destruction and loss Colorado experienced in 2012.

Colorado's Fires

When a major wildfire captures the public's attention, it can be easy to miss other fires burning. On June 23, 2012, the day the Waldo Canyon Fire began, three other fires started in Colorado. Four other large fires were already burning in Colorado during this time.

Journalist Melina Vissat was one of thousands of people evacuated from the Colorado Springs area because of the Waldo Canyon Fire. Vissat shared her experience:

> *Our house filled with smoke as I struggled to pack. What does one pack when everything is at stake? . . .*
>
> *Emergency newscasts recommended the "Four P's"— photographs, paperwork, pets, and prescriptions. I cornered the dog and cat and grabbed . . . our important papers . . . I threw clothes into a suitcase, unplugged the computer, and grabbed photo albums and wedding mementos.*
>
> *. . .*
>
> *Everything else was "replaceable."*
>
> Source: Melina Vissat. "In Fleeing Colorado Springs Fire, Tales of Kind Neighbors and Potty Breaks." Christian Science Monitor June 29, 2012. Web. Accessed January 1, 2013

Consider Your Audience

Review the excerpt closely. How would you adapt the material for a different audience, such as your parents or friends? Write a blog post giving this same information to the new audience. What is the best way to get your point across?

CHAPTER TWO

UNDERSTANDING WILDFIRES

A wildfire is an unplanned and unwanted fire that causes damage as it burns forest, shrubbery, or grass. Wildfires are sometimes called forest fires or brush fires. These terms refer to the vegetation where the fire takes place. Forest fires burn in growth taller than six feet (1.8 m). Brush fires occur in vegetation shorter than six feet (1.8 m).

A wildfire can also be called a forest fire or a brush fire, depending on the vegetation.

A surface wildfire damages trees as it burns through a forest.

There are three classes of wildfires: ground, surface, and crown. Ground fires burn on or below the floor of the forest, even down into the soil. They smolder and do not have a flame. Surface fires burn slowly along the forest floor, damaging or killing trees. This is the most common type of wildfire. Crown fires occur in treetops and spread quickly, jumping from tree to tree with the help of the wind.

The Ingredients of Fire

Fire has three ingredients: heat, fuel, and oxygen. This is called a fire triangle. Without all three parts of the triangle, or without enough of each, fire is not possible.

A heat source is needed to ignite a fire and keep it burning. Heat dries moisture in nearby fuel. It also warms the fuel and surrounding air. This helps fire travel more easily.

Fuel is anything that can burn and feed the fire. Moisture is an important factor in fuel. Material low in moisture burns more easily than material with a great deal of moisture. The size, shape, quantity, and

Oxidation

Fire is a chemical reaction called combustion. As a wildfire burns trees, brush, houses, and other fuels, it reacts with oxygen in the air. Burning wildfires consume oxygen in a process called oxidation. The oxidation process that occurs during wildfires results in heat, smoke, and embers. An ember is a small piece of burning coal or wood.

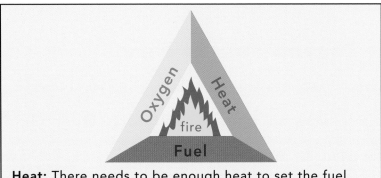

Heat: There needs to be enough heat to set the fuel on fire.
Fuel: Flammable items include dry leaves or plant roots.
Oxygen: The air we breathe.

Fire Triangle
The fire triangle represents the recipe for fire: heat, fuel, and oxygen. What happens when one of the three ingredients is missing? What happens when there is a great supply of all three ingredients?

arrangement of fuel materials across a landscape also affect a fire.

Just as humans and other living things need oxygen, so does fire. Air has approximately 21 percent oxygen. Fire needs only 16 percent oxygen to burn, so air is a great fuel for wildfires.

Fire Behavior

Weather, topography, and fuel influence a wildfire's behavior. Weather factors include temperature, wind, precipitation, and humidity. High temperatures and

Areas suffering from drought are more likely to have a wildfire.

winds can fuel wildfires. Wind can push a fire in a certain path, and fires also create their own wind currents. Precipitation and humidity can hinder wildfires by putting moisture in the air and on fuels. Lack of precipitation and humidity can allow fuels to dry out, which makes them more flammable. Areas suffering from drought become prone to wildfires.

Topography is Earth's features, such as hills and lakes. The shape of the land and location affect wildfire movement. Wildfires move faster up hills.

They are also more likely to occur on the south and west sides of hills and mountains because these tend to be drier than north and east sides.

Arrangement, moisture, and weight of fuels play a role in fire behavior. A steady layer of fuel helps wildfires spread and grow.

Forest Fire Fuels

The natural fuels that feed forest fires are aerial, surface, and ground. Aerial fuels do not touch the ground and include bark, branches, and leaves still attached to trees and bushes. Surface fuels are found on the ground and include fallen branches, leaves, cones, needles, bushes, logs, and stumps. Ground fuels are below the surface fuels. They include plant roots and rotting materials such as branches, leaves, and needles.

Studying Wildfires

Researchers explore wildfires past and present to learn how they behave and affect the environment and people. The US Geological Survey's Southern California Wildfire Risk Scenario Project studies patterns in wildfires that have reached urban areas. Researchers hope to determine why some

It is important for scientists to study past wildfires to better understand future wildfires.

communities burn while others do not. They study a variety of tools, including aerial photographs, and data about housing density and arrangement. Researchers also look at factors such as topography.

Other studies focus on what happens after wildfires occur in a certain area. After a fire destroys a neighborhood, city or state officials may change a construction code to include more fire-resistant materials. A recent study at the University of Colorado Denver asked whether government officials alter rules and laws based on what they learn from a fire.

CHAPTER THREE

CAUSES AND EFFECTS OF WILDFIRES

Wildfires can begin naturally by a lightning strike. However, people are responsible for a large percentage of wildfires. A human caused Colorado's Waldo Canyon Fire. Investigators could not determine if the fire was intentional, but arsonists have clearly caused other fires.

Although wildfires do have positive effects, the Waldo Canyon Fire is evidence that wildfires are destructive to animals, humans, and property.

Climate and Fire

The east coast of Australia, the coasts of California and Chile, and the coasts along the Mediterranean Sea are prime areas for wildfires. The reason is the climate. These regions usually have a wet season that prompts plants to grow and then a dry season that causes the new plants to dry out. The dry vegetation is good fuel for wildfires.

Negative Effects

Regardless of their cause, the effects of wildfires are the same. Land is scorched and property can be destroyed. The cost of destruction can be millions of dollars or more.

Wildfires kill animals and people. A study released in February 2012 estimated 339,000 people worldwide per year die as a result of wildfires, mostly from the smoke. In January 2013, fires ravaged Australia and Tasmania. Tens of thousands of cattle and sheep were killed.

Positive Effects

Not all effects of wildfires are negative. Wildfires act as housekeepers by cleaning the forest floor and removing underbrush. This is good for trees that

1871 Great Peshtigo Fire

Michigan

Oconto

Upper Sugar Bush

Birch Creek

Middle Sugar Bush

Menominee
Marinette

Lower Sugar Bush

Peshtigo

Door Peninsula

Oconto

Green Bay

Lake Michigan

Pensaukee

Little Suamico

Williamsonville

Sturgeon Bay

Tobinsville
New Franken

Green Bay

Brown

Kewaunee

Origin and extent of fire

Direction of wind

The Great Peshtigo Fire

Wildfires occur worldwide, and many powerful wildfires have destroyed parts of the United States. The number of acres burned and the number of lives lost are indicators of the severity of the wildfire. The Great Peshtigo Fire burned 1.2 million acres (485,622 ha) and reportedly caused 1,182 deaths. What kinds of factors do you think led to the spread of this powerful wildfire?

compete with the underbrush for valuable nutrients and space. Clearing debris opens up areas to sunlight, which is important for plant growth. Reducing heavy shrubbery relying on a river or stream can help increase the water supply. This benefits the animals

After a wildfire, new plant and tree growth will appear, which keeps a forest healthy.

and remaining plants living near the water supply since fewer plants are absorbing water.

Fires also kill bugs and diseases that can harm trees. Even with all the acres of trees lost each year to wildfires, more trees die annually because of insects and diseases. Insects kill more trees than fire, drought, wind, flooding, or disease combined. Wildfires can help keep a forest healthy.

A wildfire burn every three to 25 years is good for the health of plants. Some trees have fire-resistant bark and cones that need heat to open and reveal their seeds. Without heat from the fire, these trees cannot regenerate. Manzanita and scrub oak need the high heat from wildfires for their seeds to germinate. The leaves of these plants are naturally coated with flammable resins that encourage fire. Without fire, these plants will die out.

Even with their positive effects, wildfires are still problematic. There is no denying the destruction they cause each year. This is why firefighting is so critical.

FURTHER EVIDENCE

Chapter Three covers the causes and effects of wildfires. What was one of the chapter's key points? What evidence was provided to support this point? Visit the Web site below to learn more about the effects of forest fires. Choose a quote from the Web site that relates to this chapter. Does this quote support this chapter's main point? Does it make a new point? Write a few sentences explaining how the quote you found relates to this chapter.

Effects of Forest Fires

www.mycorelibrary.com/wildfires

CHAPTER FOUR

FIGHTING WILDFIRES

Knowing how to fight wildfires is important since they are harmful to people and animals. Firefighters battle wildfires in different ways. They fight on the ground and from the air. They use special equipment and rely on technology.

Firefighters tackle fires on the ground using different tactics. Some use fire engines with hoses. Others dig fire lines to contain the wildfire.

Fighting wildfires can be risky. Firefighters use different ways to control a wildfire.

Jobs in Firefighting

There are different types of firefighters. Fire managers decide if action is needed to control a wildfire. Handcrews work on the ground in teams of 20. They dig fire lines. The best members of handcrews move to the hotshot crew and fight large fires in high-risk locations. Helitack crews fight fires in remote areas. They arrive by helicopter and use a rope to get to the ground. Smokejumpers battle just-lit wildfires. They usually parachute to the fire. Engine crews man fire engines. Incident management teams create firefighting plans that guide firefighters. They provide supplies, such as food, water, and equipment.

They do this by removing flammable materials that act as fuel for the fire from a strip of land. Firefighters scrape the materials from the earth or dig into the soil. Without fuel, the wildfire cannot keep moving.

In addition to fire engines, firefighters use other heavy equipment. Bulldozers and tractor plows are useful for clearing vegetation. These machines are also good for building fire lines.

Firefighters use a hand tool called a Pulaski. This tool is an ax with a

Governor Christine Gregoire of Washington, *right*, holds a wildfire shelter used by firefighters in emergencies.

cutting tool called an adze. The Pulaski is helpful for chopping and grubbing, which is the act of digging up roots to create a fire line.

Fighting wildfires is risky because a wildfire can overrun firefighters. Some crews have portable fire shelters in case this happens. The shelters reflect heat and give firefighters breathable air in case a fire traps them. Although fire shelters cannot protect firefighters from all danger, they have saved lives and prevented injuries.

Firefighters sometimes work in places that are difficult to reach, such as deep in forests or high up

A helicopter carrying a Bambi Bucket helps firefighters fight a wildfire faster.

mountains. These places are often in the middle of one or more wildfires. Some firefighters reach the areas where they fight fires by helicopter or plane.

Fighting Fires from the Air

Some firefighters battle wildfires from the air using water or chemicals. Air tankers are planes fitted with tanks that carry thousands of gallons of water or flame retardant. Pilots drop their loads ahead of a wildfire on the move. When the fire reaches ground that is wet or covered with the special chemical, it dies out.

Helicopters can carry 100–2,000 gallons (379–7,571 L) of water. They carry the water in tanks or collapsible buckets called Bambi Buckets. Pilots fly to bodies of water near a fire, scoop up water in the buckets, carry it back to the fire, and drop the water on flames.

Firefighter Injuries and Deaths

Each year firefighters die on the job. From 2002 to 2011, 178 firefighters died while fighting wildfires. The most fatalities occurred in 2003, with 30. The year 2010 had the fewest, with eight. Injuries are more common than deaths in this profession. Firefighters can be injured from vehicle accidents, firefighting tools, or from slipping and falling.

Although less common, drones have been used to help track wildfires.

Fighting Fires with Technology

Technology plays a role in firefighting. Aircraft with special equipment gather information about fires. Heat data helps firefighters find the location of fires and where they might appear. Drones are unmanned aircraft that also gather heat data. This tool is less common.

Satellites and the International Space Station are also used to help fight wildfires. These resources provide information about wind and dryness that scientists use to predict where a fire will spread and how fast it will move.

Peter M. Leschak, a veteran firefighter, wrote a book about his experiences. In the passage below, Leschak discusses trying to save a house:

> Within ten or twelve minutes of the call we had eleven firefighters and all three engines on scene, and for the next two hours we sprayed and pumped, hosed and humped, heaved and chopped, shouted and laughed, battled and sweat. We did not—could not—save the house, but we neutralized the propane cylinder/bomb, snuffed the wildfire, protected an outbuilding, and toiled as a team—an elated band of brethren. Nobody got hurt. After the initial fear, and before the last grubby struggles of mop-up, it was pulse-pounding fun. It was service and duty, honorable and esteemed. Despite his loss of almost everything, the homeowner gushed in gratitude to see so many of his neighbors speed to his aid as volunteers.

> Source: Peter M. Leschak. Trials by Wildfire: In Search of the New Warrior Spirit. Duluth, MN: Pfeiffer-Hamilton, 2000. Print. 49.

Nice View

Compare Peter M. Leschak's description with the interview in Chapter One. Think about both authors' points of view. Write a short essay explaining the point of view of each document. How are they similar and why? How are they different and why?

CHAPTER FIVE

WILDFIRE PREVENTION AND SAFETY

Wildfires continue to happen, and because of their benefits, they should. However, they can be destructive, so fire prevention and safety are important for surviving a wildfire.

Campfire Safety

There are many steps people can take to reduce the risk of wildfires. When camping, it is important not to build a fire in dry conditions. Look for an existing fire

Many national and state parks post signs asking visitors to be careful and help prevent wildfires.

After a campfire, it is important to make sure you put the fire out completely.

pit rather than creating a new one. Have a shovel and a bucket of water on hand in case you need to quickly put the fire out.

It is important to put out a campfire completely. Burn the wood to ash. Pour water on the fire until it stops making a hissing sound and every ember is soaked. Stir the ashes and embers with a shovel. If water is not available, mix dirt or sand into the embers.

House Safety

People who live near wooded areas should be aware of their environment and the types of activities that can spark a fire.

Be sure to pour water on fireplace ashes before throwing them away. A lawnmower could spark a fire, so be aware of hot, dry conditions when mowing. Cigarettes can also cause fires if the ash lands on dry leaves or grass.

Keep a fire-resistant zone of at least 30 feet (9 m) around the house. This buffer zone will help protect the home from wildfires. The zone may

Tracking Wildfires

In December 2012, researchers at the University of Colorado Denver used real-time data to estimate wildfire movement. They hoped to predict a wildfire's path more quickly so people could get out of the way faster. They also wanted to guide firefighters so they could put out the fire sooner. The goal was to provide a warning similar to the kind people received when hurricanes occur, which usually gives at least a few days' notice a disaster is headed their way.

Wildfires can start from cigarettes landing on dry leaves or grass.

include plants that are fire resistant or a rock garden. Keep the roof, yard, and rain gutters free of leaves and pine needles. Fire extinguishers and garden hoses should be easy to access in case of a fire. Having your address easily identifiable from the road is also important. Firefighters will be able to find the house more quickly if they are called.

Controlled Burns

Fire experts practice wildfire prevention by setting wildfires intentionally. The US Forest Service oversees 200 million acres (80,937,128 ha) of land and uses controlled burns to prevent devastating wildfires.

This is intended to decrease large amounts of fire fuels. Controlled burns encourage new vegetation and limit the damage a wildfire can cause. Since controlled burns are relatively low-impact, low-intensity fires, they do not bring all the ecological benefits of natural wildfires.

Staying Safe When There Is a Fire

Even though people take many steps to prevent wildfires, they will still happen. It is important to know how to stay safe and prepare for evacuation.

Smoke can be dangerous if inhaled. It can cause coughing, a scratchy throat, shortness

Doubts about Controlled Burns

Some scientists question the use of controlled burns. Some ecologists and environmentalists argue controlled fires do not prevent bigger fires. Instead, some scientists support a free-fire model. These people believe major fires are needed for biodiversity and view widespread wildfires as necessary for wildlife and the environment.

Researchers hope their work will limit future destruction from wildfires.

of breath, headaches, a runny nose, and stinging eyes. Watch for air-quality updates and stay indoors.

When officials say it is time to evacuate, there are many steps to follow. Have your parent or guardian park the car close to the house for a quick escape. Important documents and items should be put in the car. The adults should make sure the garden hose is hooked up and working. You can help your parents or guardians fill containers around the house, such as swimming pools and garbage cans, with water. An adult can also set sprinklers on the roof and turn them on.

Researchers continue to learn about wildfires. Experts know ways to prevent fires, fight fires, and stay safe when fires occur. People can use this knowledge to better limit the loss wildfires cause and increase the growth and biodiversity they promote.

EXPLORE ONLINE

Chapter Five has information about wildfire safety and prevention. There are many steps people can take to keep wildfires from starting and spreading. People can also take precautions to stay safe if a wildfire is nearby. The Web site below lists safety tips to prepare for a wildfire. As you know, every source is different. How is the information given on this Web site different from the facts in this chapter? What information is the same? What can you learn from this Web site?

Preparing for Wildfires
www.mycorelibrary.com/wildfires

TEN DESTRUCTIVE WILDFIRES

October 8, 1871
Upper Peninsula, Michigan
The Peshtigo Fire burned 1.2 million acres (485,622 ha) in northern Wisconsin and the Upper Peninsula of Michigan. It is believed to have killed more people than any other US fire.

August 20–21, 1910
Idaho, Montana, and Washington
The Big Burn consumed 3 million acres (1.2 million ha) of land in Idaho, Montana, and Washington. Eighty-five lives were lost. It is considered the largest wildfire in United States history.

October 12, 1918
Cloquet, Minnesota
Sparked by a train engine, the Cloquet Fire in Minnesota burned 250,000 acres (101,171 ha), killed 453 people, and destroyed 52,000 homes.

January 13, 1939
Australia
Almost 5 million acres (2 million ha) burned and at least 71 people died because of the Black Friday Brushfires in Australia.

August 5, 1949
Montana
While trying to fight the Mann Gulch Fire in Montana, 16 firefighters soon needed to escape a dangerous situation. Thirteen of them died and 5,000 acres (2,023 ha) ultimately burned.

May 6, 1987
China
The Daxing'anling Wildfire in China was not the first wildfire in the Daxing'anling Mountains, but it was the worst. It burned for almost a month, destroying more than 2 million acres (971,245 ha), killing more than 200 people, and leaving more than 50,000 homeless.

October 1997
Indonesia
Believed to be the largest fire in the world's history, the Indonesia wildfire destroyed almost 20 million acres (8 million ha) of land. An unknown number of lives were lost.

October 2003
California
The Cedar Fire burned more than 750,000 acres (303,514 ha) in southern California and killed 14 people. It was started after a lost hiker started a small fire to alert rescuers.

Summer 2007
Greece
Greece lost 84 people and 670,000 acres (271,139 ha) in the summer of 2007 to wildfires. A farmer admitted to starting some of them and was sentenced to prison for his actions.

February 7, 2009
Victoria, Australia
Hundreds of wildfires burned in Victoria, Australia, in early 2009. The fires ruined 1.1 million acres (445,154 ha) and killed 173 people.

Why Do I Care?

This book discusses how wildfires have affected many people's lives. Even if you live in an area that is unlikely to experience a wildfire, how do the victims' experiences connect to your life? Maybe you have experienced another weather-related disaster. Write down two or three ways a wildfire victim's experiences connect to your life.

Another View

There are many different sources about wildfires. Each source is a little bit different. Ask a librarian or another adult to help you find a reliable source on wildfires. Then write a short essay comparing and contrasting the new source's point of view to the ideas in this book. How are the sources different? How are the sources similar? Why do you think they are different or similar?

Take a Stand

Take a position on the use of controlled burning. Write a brief essay explaining your opinion. Make sure you give reasons for your opinion. Give some evidence to support those reasons.

Tell the Tale

Chapter Two discusses several terrible wildfires. Pick one of the wildfires listed. Write 200 words describing the true story of this event. Be sure to set the scene, develop a sequence of events, and offer a conclusion.

GLOSSARY

adze
a cutting tool with a curved blade that is used to shape wood

arsonist
a person who sets a fire intentionally

biodiversity
animal and plant species found in a particular environment

embers
the smoking remains of a fire

fire line
a line of land that has been cleared or dug up to stop a fire from advancing

fire retardant
a chemical dropped on a fire to put it out or keep it from advancing

germinate
to cause to sprout

grubbing
digging up roots to clear the way

Pulaski
an ax that has a long back shaped like an adze

resin
a yellowish or brownish substance that comes from a plant

smolder
to burn slowly without a flame

underbrush
shrubs and small trees that grow in forests between the large trees

LEARN MORE

Books

Hamilton, John. *Wildfires*. Edina, MN: ABDO, 2005.

Linton, Jeremy V., ed. *Wildfires: Issues and Consequences*. Hauppauge, NY: Nova Science Publishers, 2004.

Trammel, Howard K. *Wildfires*. New York, NY: Scholastic, 2009.

Web Links

To learn more about wildfires, visit ABDO Publishing Company online at **www.abdopublishing.com**. Web sites about wildfires are featured on our Book Links page. These links are routinely monitored and updated to provide the most current information available.

Visit **www.mycorelibrary.com** for teachers and students.

INDEX

ABOUT THE AUTHOR

Rebecca Rowell has written several books for young readers. She has a Master of Arts in Publishing and Writing from Emerson College and lives in Minnesota with her three cats.